Sunday SUPPERS

D0150782

Supper Sides 2

Comforting Casseroles 14

Hearty Family Favorites 28

Old-Fashioned Desserts 44

Weeknight Dinner Solutions 62

Kitchen Sense 76

Tailgating Fun 78

Acknowledgments 95

Index 96

Supper
S·I·D·E·S

Broccoli Casserole with Crumb Topping

▋▋▋

- 2 slices day-old white bread, coarsely crumbled (about 1¼ cups)
- ½ cup shredded mozzarella cheese (about 2 ounces)
- 2 tablespoons chopped fresh parsley (optional)
- 2 tablespoons olive or vegetable oil
- 1 clove garlic, finely chopped
- 6 cups broccoli florets and/or cauliflowerets
- 1 envelope LIPTON® RECIPE SECRETS® Onion Soup Mix*
- 1 cup water
- 1 large tomato, chopped

*Also terrific with LIPTON® RECIPE SECRETS® Garlic Mushroom Soup Mix.

1. In small bowl, combine bread crumbs, cheese, parsley, 1 tablespoon oil and garlic; set aside.

2. In 12-inch skillet, heat remaining 1 tablespoon oil over medium heat and cook broccoli, stirring frequently, 2 minutes.

3. Stir in soup mix blended with water. Bring to a boil over high heat. Reduce heat to low and simmer uncovered, stirring occasionally, 8 minutes or until broccoli is almost tender. Add tomato and simmer 2 minutes.

4. Spoon vegetable mixture into 1½-quart casserole; top with bread crumb mixture. Broil 1½ minutes or until crumbs are golden and cheese is melted.

Makes 6 servings

Garden Vegetable Salad

▌▌▌

⅔ cup red wine vinegar
½ cup WESSON® Vegetable Oil
1½ tablespoons fresh lemon
   juice
1 teaspoon prepared
   horseradish
1 teaspoon fresh minced
   garlic
½ teaspoon salt
¼ teaspoon coarsely ground
   black pepper
2 cups peeled and thinly
   sliced carrots (¼ inch
   thick)
1½ cups thinly sliced zucchini
   (¼ inch thick)
2 medium red onions, sliced
   and separated into rings
1 cup cherry tomatoes,
   halved
½ cup julienned red bell
   pepper
⅓ cup crumbled blue cheese
2 tablespoons chopped fresh
   basil
2 tablespoons chopped fresh
   parsley
1 tablespoon snipped chives

In a small bowl, combine *first*
7 ingredients, ending with black
pepper. Whisk vigorously until
well blended; set aside. In a
large bowl, combine carrots,
zucchini, onions, tomatoes, bell
pepper, *half* the blue cheese,
basil and parsley. Pour dressing
over vegetables; toss until well
coated. Cover and refrigerate
at least 2 hours, stirring
occasionally. Stir once more
before serving. Sprinkle
remaining cheese and chives
over salad.   *Makes 8 servings*

Mandarin Orange and Red Onion Salad

▌▌▌

1 cup BLUE DIAMOND® Sliced
   Natural Almonds
1 tablespoon butter
2 tablespoons lemon juice
1 teaspoon Dijon mustard
½ teaspoon sugar
½ teaspoon salt
¼ teaspoon white pepper
½ cup vegetable oil
1 head romaine lettuce, torn
   into pieces
1 can (11 ounces) mandarin
   orange segments, drained
1 small red onion, thinly
   sliced, rings separated

Sauté almonds in butter until
golden; reserve. Combine
lemon juice, mustard, sugar,
salt and pepper in small bowl.
Whisk in oil. Combine lettuce,
oranges, onion and almonds.
Toss with dressing.
      Makes 4 to 6 servings

Garden Vegetable Salad

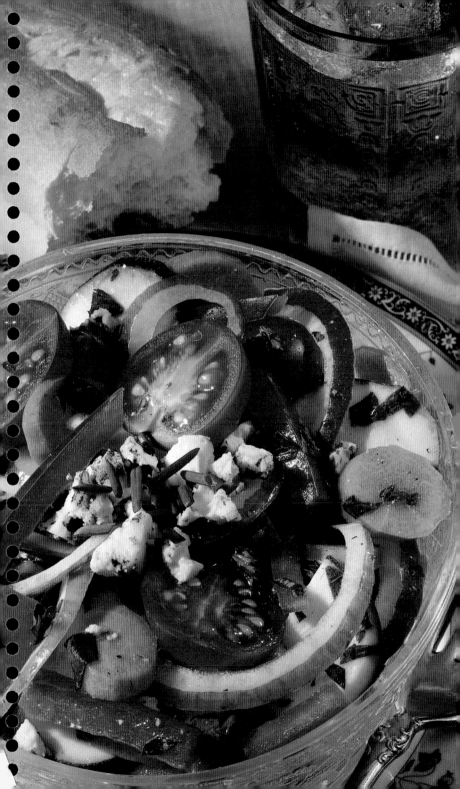

Roasted Mixed Vegetables

▌▌▌

4 large red skin potatoes, cut
    into wedges (about
    2 pounds)
3 large carrots, peeled and
    cut into 1½-inch pieces
    (about 2 cups)
3 large parsnips, peeled and
    cut into 1½-inch pieces
    (about 2 cups)
2 large onions, cut into
    wedges
1 tablespoon dried rosemary
    leaves
2 teaspoons garlic powder
¼ cup FLEISCHMANN'S®
    Original Margarine,
    melted

1. Mix potatoes, carrots,
parsnips and onions with
rosemary and garlic powder
in large bowl.

2. Drizzle with melted
margarine, tossing to coat well.
Spread in a 13×9×2-inch
baking pan.

3. Bake at 450°F for 40 to
45 minutes or until fork-tender,
stirring occasionally.
                Makes 8 servings

Prep Time: 15 minutes
Cook Time: 40 minutes
Total Time: 55 minutes

Swanson® Glazed Snow Peas & Carrots

▌▌▌

4 teaspoons cornstarch
1 can (14½ ounces)
    SWANSON® Vegetable
    Broth
4 medium carrots, sliced
    (about 2 cups)
1 medium onion, chopped
    (about ½ cup)
¾ pound snow peas (about
    4 cups)
1 teaspoon lemon juice

1. In measuring cup, mix
cornstarch and *1 cup* broth
until smooth. Set aside.

2. In medium skillet over high
heat, heat remaining broth to
a boil. Add carrots and onion.
Reduce heat to medium. Cover
and cook 5 minutes or until
carrots are tender-crisp. Add
snow peas. Cook 2 minutes.

3. Stir cornstarch mixture and
add to carrot mixture. Cook
until mixture boils and
thickens, stirring constantly.
Stir in lemon juice.
                Makes 8 servings

Prep Time: 15 minutes
Cook Time: 10 minutes

Roasted Mixed Vegetables

Twice Baked Ranch Potatoes

▮▮▮

4 baking potatoes
½ cup KRAFT® Ranch Dressing
¼ cup BREAKSTONE'S® or
　　KNUDSEN® Sour Cream
1 tablespoon OSCAR MAYER®
　　Real Bacon Bits
¼ pound (4 ounces)
　　VELVEETA® Pasteurized
　　Prepared Cheese
　　Product, cut up

1. Bake potatoes at 400°F for 1 hour. Slice off tops of potatoes; scoop out centers, leaving ⅛-inch shell.

2. Mash potatoes. Add dressing, sour cream and bacon bits; beat until fluffy. Stir Velveeta into potato mixture. Spoon into shells.

3. Bake at 350°F for 20 minutes.
Makes 4 servings

How to Bake Potatoes: Russet potatoes are best for baking. Scrub potatoes well, blot dry and rub the skin with a little oil and salt. Prick the skin of the potatoes with a fork so steam can escape. Stand them on end in a muffin tin. Bake at 400°F for 60 minutes or until tender.

Prep Time: 20 minutes plus baking potatoes
Bake Time: 20 minutes

Spinach, Cheese & Walnut Salad

▮▮▮

1 package (8 ounces) cream
　　cheese
1 cup walnuts, chopped
½ pound fresh spinach,
　　washed and drained
3 stalks celery, sliced
1 piece cucumber (about
　　2 inches), diced
1 Granny Smith or red apple,
　　cored and diced
¼ cup lemon juice
¼ cup walnut or safflower oil
　　Salt and black pepper to
　　taste

Roll cheese into balls, using about 1 teaspoon cheese for each ball. Lightly roll balls in chopped walnuts. Refrigerate cheese balls until ready to serve. Remove stems from spinach and tear leaves into bite-size pieces. Combine spinach, celery and cucumber in serving bowl. Toss apple in lemon juice in small bowl; add apple to spinach mixture, reserving lemon juice. Blend oil, salt and pepper into reserved lemon juice; pour over spinach mixture. Toss to coat. Just before serving, place cheese balls in salad.
Makes 4 servings

Twice Baked Ranch Potatoes

Green Beans and Shiitake Mushrooms

▌▌▌

10 to 12 dried shiitake mushrooms (about 1 ounce)
¾ cup water, divided
3 tablespoons oyster sauce
1 tablespoon cornstarch
4 cloves garlic, minced
⅛ teaspoon red pepper flakes
1 tablespoon vegetable oil
¾ to 1 pound fresh green beans, ends trimmed
⅓ cup slivered fresh basil leaves or chopped cilantro
2 green onions, sliced diagonally
⅓ cup roasted peanuts (optional)

1. Place mushrooms in small bowl; cover with hot water. Let stand 30 minutes or until caps are soft. Drain mushrooms; squeeze out excess water. Remove and discard stems. Slice caps into thin strips.

2. Combine ¼ cup water, oyster sauce, cornstarch, garlic and red pepper in small bowl; mix well. Set aside.

3. Heat wok or medium skillet over medium-high heat. Add oil and swirl to coat surface. Add mushrooms, beans and remaining ½ cup water; cook and stir until water boils. Reduce heat to medium-low; cover and cook 8 to 10 minutes or until beans are crisp-tender, stirring occasionally.

4. Stir cornstarch mixture; add to wok. Cook and stir until sauce thickens and coats beans. (If cooking water has evaporated, add enough water to form thick sauce.) Stir in basil, green onions and peanuts, if desired; mix well. Transfer to serving platter. Garnish as desired.

Makes 4 to 6 servings

Cook's Notes

Shiitake mushrooms are wild mushrooms from Japan that are easily cultivated. Their woodsy odor and rich, smoky mushroom flavor contribute to their popularity.

Green Beans and Shiitake Mushrooms

Georgia-Style Lemon Pilaf

▌▌▌

¼ cup WESSON® Vegetable Oil
½ cup minced sweet onion
½ cup diced celery
1 cup uncooked long-grain rice
1 (14½-ounce) can chicken broth
½ cup water
⅓ cup dried currants
2 tablespoons fresh lemon juice
2 teaspoons grated fresh lemon peel
¼ cup sliced almonds, toasted
1 tablespoon fresh chopped parsley

In a large saucepan, heat Wesson® Oil until hot. Add onion and celery; sauté until crisp-tender. Add rice; continue sautéing an additional 3 minutes. Mix in *remaining* ingredients *except* almonds and parsley. Bring mixture to a boil, stirring occasionally. Cover, reduce heat to medium-low and cook until liquid is absorbed and rice is tender, about 20 minutes. Mix in almonds and parsley; cover and let stand 5 minutes. Fluff with fork before serving.

Makes 4 servings

Roasted Idaho & Sweet Potatoes

▌▌▌

1 envelope LIPTON® RECIPE SECRETS® Onion Soup Mix
2 medium all-purpose potatoes, peeled, if desired, and cut into large chunks (about 1 pound)
2 medium sweet potatoes or yams, peeled, if desired, and cut into large chunks (about 1 pound)
¼ cup olive or vegetable oil

1. Preheat oven to 425°F. In large plastic food storage bag or bowl, add all ingredients. Close bag and shake, or toss in bowl, until potatoes are evenly coated.

2. In 13×9-inch baking or roasting pan, arrange potatoes; discard bag.

3. Bake uncovered, stirring occasionally, 40 minutes or until potatoes are tender and golden.   *Makes 4 servings*

Cranberry-Raisin Stuffing

▌▌▌

12 slices cinnamon-raisin
    bread, toasted
½ cup butter or margarine
2½ cups chopped onions
1 teaspoon rubbed sage
1 bag (12 ounces) fresh or
    partially thawed frozen
    cranberries, washed,
    picked through and
    coarsely chopped
¼ cup sugar
¼ to ½ cup chicken broth*

*If baking stuffing in casserole dish, use
½ cup chicken broth and bake, covered,
at 350°F for 45 minutes or until heated
through.*

Cut toast into ½-inch cubes.
Place in large bowl; set aside.
Melt butter in large skillet; add
onions. Cook and stir about
10 minutes or until tender.
Add sage; cook 1 minute more.
Toss cranberries with sugar
in medium bowl. Add onion
mixture and cranberries to
bread cubes; mix well. Pour
¼ cup chicken broth over bread
cube mixture; mix until evenly
moistened. Stuff body and neck
of turkey and cook according to
instructions given with turkey.
Makes 7½ cups stuffing

Creamed Spinach

▌▌▌

3 cups water
2 bags (10 ounces each)
    fresh spinach, washed,
    stems removed and
    chopped
2 teaspoons margarine
2 tablespoons all-purpose
    flour
1 cup fat-free (skim) milk
2 tablespoons grated
    Parmesan cheese
⅛ teaspoon white pepper
  Ground nutmeg

1. Bring water to a boil; add
spinach. Reduce heat and
simmer, covered, about
5 minutes or until spinach is
wilted. Drain well. Set aside.

2. Melt margarine in small
saucepan; stir in flour and
cook over medium-low heat
1 minute, stirring constantly.
Using wire whisk, stir in milk;
bring to a boil. Cook, whisking
constantly, 1 to 2 minutes or
until mixture thickens. Stir in
cheese and pepper.

3. Stir spinach into sauce; heat
thoroughly. Spoon into serving
bowl; sprinkle lightly with
nutmeg. Garnish as desired.
Makes 4 servings

Comforting CASSEROLES

Chicken & Biscuits

▪▪▪

¼ cup butter or margarine
4 boneless skinless chicken
    breasts (about
    1¼ pounds), cut into
    ½-inch pieces
½ cup chopped onion
½ teaspoon dried thyme
    leaves
½ teaspoon paprika
¼ teaspoon black pepper
1 can (about 14 ounces)
    chicken broth, divided
⅓ cup all-purpose flour
1 package (10 ounces) frozen
    peas and carrots
1 can (12 ounces)
    refrigerated biscuits

1. Preheat oven to 375°F. Melt butter in large skillet over medium heat. Add chicken, onion, thyme, paprika and pepper. Cook 5 minutes or until chicken is browned.

2. Combine ¼ cup chicken broth with flour; stir until smooth. Set aside.

3. Add remaining chicken broth to skillet; bring to a boil. Gradually add flour mixture, stirring constantly to prevent lumps from forming. Simmer 5 minutes. Add peas and carrots; continue cooking 2 minutes.

4. Transfer to 1½-quart casserole; top with biscuits. Bake 25 to 30 minutes or until biscuits are golden brown.
Makes 4 to 6 servings

Tip: Use an ovenproof skillet to cook chicken in and omit the 1½-quart casserole. Place biscuits directly on chicken and vegetable mixture and bake as directed.

Tuscan Pot Pie

▌▌▌

¾ **pound sweet or hot Italian
sausage**
1 **jar (26 to 28 ounces)
prepared chunky
vegetable or mushroom
spaghetti sauce**
1 **can (19 ounces) cannellini
beans, rinsed and drained**
½ **teaspoon dried thyme
leaves**
1½ **cups (6 ounces) shredded
mozzarella cheese**
1 **package (8 ounces)
refrigerated crescent
dinner rolls**

1. Preheat oven to 425°F.
Remove sausage from casings.
Brown sausage in medium
ovenproof skillet, stirring to
separate meat. Drain drippings.

2. Add spaghetti sauce, beans
and thyme to skillet. Simmer
uncovered over medium heat
5 minutes. Remove from heat;
stir in cheese.

3. Unroll crescent dough;
divide into triangles. Arrange in
spiral with points of dough
towards center, covering
sausage mixture completely.
Bake 12 minutes or until crust
is golden brown and meat
mixture is bubbly.
Makes 4 to 6 servings

Beef & Artichoke Casserole

▌▌▌

¾ **pound ground beef**
½ **cup sliced mushrooms**
¼ **cup chopped onion**
1 **clove garlic, minced**
1 **can (14 ounces) artichoke
hearts, drained, chopped**
½ **cup dry bread crumbs**
¼ **cup (1 ounce) grated
Parmesan cheese**
1 **teaspoon dried rosemary**
½ **teaspoon dried marjoram
leaves**
 Salt and black pepper
3 **egg whites**

1. Preheat oven to 400°F. Spray
1-quart casserole with nonstick
cooking spray.

2. Brown ground beef in skillet,
stirring to break up meat; drain.
Add mushrooms, onion and
garlic; cook until tender.

3. Mix beef mixture, artichokes,
crumbs, cheese, rosemary and
marjoram; mix lightly. Season
with salt and pepper to taste.

4. Beat egg whites until stiff
peaks form; fold into beef
mixture. Spoon into prepared
casserole. Bake 20 minutes or
until browned around edges.
Makes 4 servings

Tuscan Pot Pie

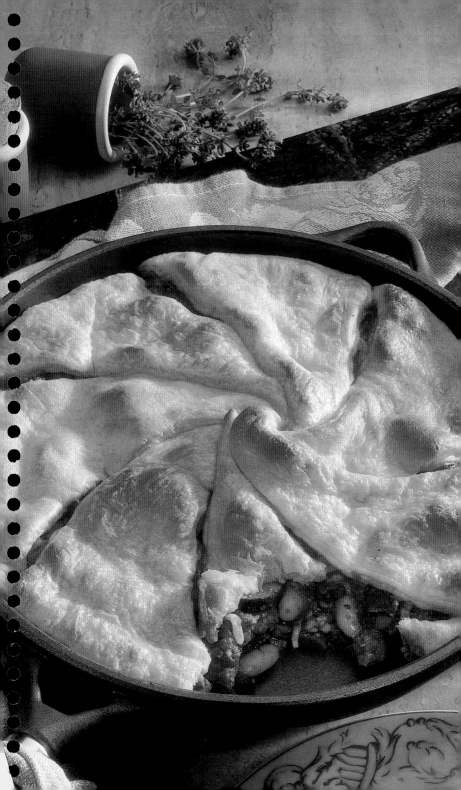

Creamy Chicken and Pasta with Spinach

▮▮▮

6 ounces uncooked egg
   noodles
1 tablespoon olive oil
¼ cup chopped onion
¼ cup chopped red bell
   pepper
1 package (10 ounces) frozen
   spinach, thawed and
   drained
2 boneless skinless chicken
   breasts (¾ pound),
   cooked and cut into
   1-inch pieces
1 can (4 ounces) sliced
   mushrooms, drained
2 cups (8 ounces) shredded
   Swiss cheese
1 container (8 ounces) sour
   cream
¾ cup half-and-half
2 eggs, lightly beaten
½ teaspoon salt
   Red onion and fresh
   spinach for garnish

1. Preheat oven to 350°F. Prepare noodles according to package directions; set aside.

2. Heat oil in large skillet over medium-high heat. Add onion and bell pepper; cook and stir 2 minutes or until onion is tender. Add spinach, chicken, mushrooms and cooked noodles; stir to combine.

3. Combine cheese, sour cream, half-and-half, eggs and salt in medium bowl; blend well.

4. Add cheese mixture to chicken mixture; stir to combine. Pour into 13×9-inch baking dish coated with nonstick cooking spray. Bake, covered, 30 to 35 minutes or until heated through. Garnish with red onion and fresh spinach, if desired.

Makes 8 servings

Cook's Nook

For best results when draining thawed frozen spinach, press the spinach between two nested pie plates, tilting the plates over the sink to drain well.

*Creamy Chicken and
Pasta with Spinach*

Reuben Noodle Bake

▋▋▋

8 ounces uncooked egg
  noodles
5 ounces thinly sliced deli-
  style corned beef,
  chopped
1 can (14½ ounces)
  sauerkraut with caraway
  seeds, drained
2 cups (8 ounces) shredded
  Swiss cheese
½ cup Thousand Island
  dressing
½ cup milk
1 tablespoon prepared
  mustard
2 slices pumpernickel bread
1 tablespoon butter, melted

Preheat oven to 350°F. Spray
13×9-inch baking dish with
nonstick cooking spray. Cook
noodles according to package
directions until al dente. Drain.
Mix noodles, corned beef,
sauerkraut and cheese in large
bowl. Spread in prepared dish.
Mix dressing, milk and mustard
in small bowl; spoon evenly
over noodle mixture. Tear bread
into large pieces. Process in
food processor until crumbs
form. Mix bread crumbs and
butter in small bowl; sprinkle
evenly over casserole. Bake,
uncovered, 25 to 30 minutes or
until heated through.
Makes 6 servings

Turnip Shepherd's Pie

▋▋▋

1 pound small turnips, peeled
  and cut into ½-inch cubes
1 pound lean ground turkey
⅓ cup dry bread crumbs
¼ cup chopped onion
¼ cup ketchup
1 egg
½ teaspoon salt
½ teaspoon black pepper
⅓ cup half-and-half
1 tablespoon butter
1 tablespoon chopped fresh
  parsley
¼ cup shredded sharp
  Cheddar cheese

Preheat oven to 400°F. Place
turnips in saucepan; cover with
water. Cover and bring to a boil;
reduce heat to medium-low.
Simmer 20 minutes or until
fork-tender. Mix turkey, crumbs,
onion, ketchup, egg, salt and
pepper. Pat on bottom and side
of 9-inch pie pan. Bake 20 to
30 minutes until turkey is no
longer pink. Drain cooked
turnips. Mash turnips until
smooth; blend in half-and-half
and butter. Season with salt and
pepper to taste. Fill shell with
turnip mixture; sprinkle with
parsley, then cheese. Return to
oven until cheese melts.
Makes 4 servings

Reuben Noodle Bake

Tuna Noodle Casserole

▮▮▮

7 ounces uncooked macaroni
2 tablespoons butter
¾ cup chopped onion
½ cup thinly sliced celery
½ cup chopped red pepper
2 tablespoons all-purpose flour
1 teaspoon salt
⅛ teaspoon white pepper
1½ cups milk
1 can (6 ounces) albacore tuna in water, drained
½ cup grated Parmesan cheese, divided

Preheat oven to 375°F. Spray 8-inch square baking dish with nonstick cooking spray. Cook pasta according to package directions until al dente. Drain; set aside. Melt butter in skillet over medium heat. Add onion; cook and stir 3 minutes. Add celery and red pepper; cook and stir 3 minutes. Sprinkle flour, salt and white pepper over vegetables; cook and stir 1 minute. Stir in milk; cook and stir until thickened. Remove from heat. Add pasta, tuna and ¼ cup cheese to skillet; stir until pasta is well coated. Pour tuna mixture into prepared dish; sprinkle with remaining ¼ cup cheese. Bake uncovered 20 to 25 minutes or until hot and bubbly. *Makes 4 servings*

Spinach-Potato Bake

▮▮▮

1 pound ground beef
2 cloves garlic, minced
½ cup sliced fresh mushrooms
1 small onion, chopped
1 package (10 ounces) frozen chopped spinach, thawed, well drained
½ teaspoon ground nutmeg
1 pound russet potatoes, peeled, cooked, mashed
¼ cup light sour cream
¼ cup fat-free (skim) milk
Salt and black pepper
½ cup (2 ounces) shredded Cheddar cheese

1. Preheat oven to 400°F. Spray deep 9-inch casserole dish with nonstick cooking spray.

2. Cook and stir beef in skillet, until browned; drain. Add garlic, mushrooms and onion; cook until tender. Add spinach and nutmeg; cook and stir until hot.

3. Mix potatoes, sour cream and milk. Add to beef mixture; season with salt and pepper to taste. Spoon into prepared casserole; sprinkle with cheese.

4. Bake 15 to 20 minutes or until slightly puffed and cheese is melted. *Makes 6 servings*

Tuna Noodle Casserole

Mexican Lasagna

▮▮▮

2 tablespoons vegetable oil
4 boneless skinless chicken
    breast halves, cut into
    ½-inch pieces
2 teaspoons chili powder
1 teaspoon ground cumin
1 can (14½ ounces) diced
    tomatoes with garlic,
    drained
1 can (8 ounces) tomato
    sauce
1 teaspoon hot pepper sauce
1 cup ricotta cheese
1 can (4 ounces) diced green
    chilies
¼ cup chopped fresh cilantro,
    divided
12 (6-inch) corn tortillas
1 cup (4 ounces) shredded
    Cheddar cheese

Preheat oven to 375°F. Heat oil in skillet over medium heat. Add chicken, chili powder and cumin. Cook and stir 4 minutes or until tender. Stir in tomatoes, tomato sauce and pepper sauce; bring to a boil. Reduce heat; simmer 2 minutes. Mix ricotta, chilies and half of cilantro in bowl until blended. Spoon half of chicken mixture into 12×8-inch baking dish. Top with 6 tortillas, cheese mixture, remaining 6 tortillas, remaining chicken mixture, Cheddar cheese and remaining cilantro. Bake 25 minutes or until hot.

Makes 6 to 8 servings

Broccoli-Rice Casserole

▮▮▮

½ cup chopped onion
½ cup chopped celery
⅓ cup chopped red pepper
1 can (10¾ ounces)
    condensed broccoli and
    cheese soup
¼ cup sour cream
2 cups cooked rice
1 package (10 ounces) frozen
    chopped broccoli, thawed
    and drained
1 tomato, sliced ¼ inch thick

1. Preheat oven to 350°F. Coat 1½-quart baking dish with nonstick cooking spray; set aside.

2. Coat skillet with cooking spray. Add onion, celery and pepper; cook and stir over medium heat until crisp-tender. Stir in soup and sour cream. Layer rice and broccoli in prepared dish. Top with soup mixture, spreading evenly.

3. Cover and bake 20 minutes. Top with tomato slices; bake, uncovered, 10 minutes.

Makes 6 servings

Mexican Lasagna

Sweet Potato and Apple Casserole

■ ■ ■

4 tablespoons butter, divided
½ cup packed dark brown sugar
½ teaspoon ground cinnamon
¼ teaspoon ground mace or nutmeg
2 pounds fresh sweet potatoes, peeled, sliced in half lengthwise and cut crosswise into ½-inch slices
Salt
2 Granny Smith apples, peeled, quartered and cored
½ cup granola cereal

1. Preheat oven to 375°F. Grease 2-quart casserole or baking pan with 1 tablespoon butter. Mix brown sugar, cinnamon and mace in small bowl. Place ⅓ of potato slices in bottom of prepared casserole. Sprinkle with salt to taste. Crumble half the sugar mixture over potatoes and dot with 1 tablespoon butter.

2. Slice each apple quarter into four wedges. Layer half the apples on top of potatoes in casserole. Repeat layers. Top with remaining potatoes and 1 tablespoon butter. Cover with lid or aluminum foil.

3. Bake 25 minutes. Uncover; spoon pan liquid over potatoes. Sprinkle with granola; bake 35 minutes more or until potatoes are fork-tender. Garnish, if desired.

Makes 6 side-dish servings

Cook's Notes

Mace is the red membrane that covers the nutmeg seed. It has a yellow-orange color when dried and is usually sold in ground form. Mace smells and tastes like a stronger version of nutmeg.

Sweet Potato and Apple Casserole

Hearty Family
FAVORITES

Herb Roasted Turkey

▮▮▮

1 (12-pound) turkey, thawed if frozen
½ cup FLEISCHMANN'S® Original Margarine, softened, divided
1 tablespoon Italian seasoning

1. Remove neck and giblets from turkey cavities. Rinse turkey; drain well and pat dry. Free legs from tucked position; do not cut band of skin. Using rubber spatula or hand, loosen skin over breast, starting at body cavity opening by legs.

2. Combine 6 tablespoons margarine and Italian seasoning. Spread 2 tablespoons herb mixture inside body cavity; spread remaining herb mixture on meat under skin. Hold skin in place at opening with wooden picks. Return legs to tucked position; turn wings back to hold neck skin in place.

3. Place turkey, breast-side up, on flat rack in shallow open pan. Insert meat thermometer deep into thickest part of thigh next to body, not touching bone. Melt remaining 2 tablespoons margarine; brush over skin.

4. Roast at 325°F for 3½ to 3¾ hours. When skin is golden brown, shield breast loosely with foil to prevent overbrowning. Check for doneness; thigh temperature should be 180° to 185°F. Let turkey stand 15 to 20 minutes before carving.

Makes 12 servings

Prep Time: 20 minutes
Cook Time: 3 hours 30 minutes
Cool Time: 15 minutes
Total Time: 4 hours 5 minutes

Pork Chops and Apple Stuffing Bake

▌▌▌

6 (¾-inch-thick) boneless
   pork loin chops (about
   1½ pounds)
¼ teaspoon salt
⅛ teaspoon black pepper
1 tablespoon vegetable oil
1 small onion, chopped
2 ribs celery, chopped
2 Granny Smith apples,
   peeled and coarsely
   chopped (about 2 cups)
1 can (14½ ounces) reduced-
   sodium chicken broth
1 can (10¾ ounces)
   condensed cream of
   celery soup
¼ cup dry white wine
6 cups herb-seasoned stuffing
   cubes

1. Preheat oven to 375°F. Spray 13×9-inch baking dish with nonstick cooking spray.

2. Season both sides of pork chops with salt and pepper. Heat oil in large deep skillet over medium-high heat until hot. Add chops and cook until browned on both sides, turning once. Remove chops from skillet; set aside.

3. Add onion and celery to same skillet. Cook and stir 3 minutes or until onion is tender. Add apples; cook and stir 1 minute. Add broth, soup and wine; mix well. Bring to a simmer; remove from heat. Stir in stuffing cubes until evenly moistened.

4. Spread stuffing mixture evenly in prepared dish. Place pork chops on top of stuffing; pour any accumulated juices over chops. Cover tightly with foil and bake 30 to 40 minutes or until pork chops are juicy and barely pink in center.

Makes 6 servings

Cook's Nook

Crisp, tart, juicy Granny Smith apples are not only delicious eaten raw, but are also excellent for baking because they keep their shape and texture. Apples will keep in a cool, dry place for a week or two. For longer storage, place apples in a plastic bag and store in the refrigerator. Apples in good condition can last up to six weeks in the refrigerator. Check them occasionally and discard any that have begun to spoil as one rotten apple can ruin the whole lot.

Peppered Beef Tip Roast

▌▌▌

1 (3½- to 5-pound) beef tip
    roast
2 teaspoons *each* cracked
    black pepper and dry
    mustard
½ teaspoon *each* ground
    allspice and ground red
    pepper
1 large clove garlic, minced
1 teaspoon vegetable oil

Combine black pepper, dry
mustard, allspice, red pepper
and garlic; stir in oil to form
paste. Spread mixture evenly on
surface of beef tip roast. Place
roast, fat side up, on rack in
open roasting pan. Insert meat
thermometer so bulb is
centered in thickest part. Do
not add water. Do not cover.
Roast in 325°F oven to
desired doneness. Allow 30 to
35 minutes per pound. Remove
roast when meat thermometer
registers 135°F for rare; 155°F
for medium. Allow roast to
stand 15 to 20 minutes in a
warm place for carving. Roast
will continue to rise about 5°F
in temperature to reach 140°F
for rare; 160°F for medium.
*Makes 2 to 4 servings per
pound*

Favorite recipe from **National
Cattlemen's Beef Association**

Italian-Style Meat Loaf

▌▌▌

1 can (6 ounces) tomato
    paste
½ cup dry red wine
½ cup water
1 teaspoon minced garlic
½ teaspoon dried basil leaves
½ teaspoon dried oregano
    leaves
¼ teaspoon salt
12 ounces lean ground round
12 ounces ground turkey
    breast
1 cup fresh bread crumbs
    (2 slices bread)
½ cup shredded zucchini
¼ cup egg substitute *or* 2 egg
    whites

1. Preheat oven to 350°F. Mix
tomato paste, wine, water,
garlic, basil, oregano and salt in
saucepan. Bring to a boil; reduce
heat to low. Simmer, uncovered,
15 minutes; set aside.

2. Mix beef, turkey, bread
crumbs, zucchini, egg
substitute and ½ cup tomato
mixture in bowl. Mix well.
Shape into loaf; place in
ungreased 9×5×3-inch loaf
pan. Bake 45 minutes. Discard
any drippings. Pour ½ cup
remaining tomato mixture over
top of loaf. Bake 15 minutes.
Place on serving platter. Cool
10 minutes before cutting into
8 slices.　　*Makes 8 servings*

Glazed Roast Pork Loin with Cranberry Stuffing

▐ ▐ ▐

1¼ cups chopped fresh or
    partially thawed frozen
    cranberries
2 teaspoons sugar
½ cup butter or margarine
1 cup chopped onion
1 package (8 ounces) herb-
    seasoned stuffing mix
1 cup chicken broth
½ cup peeled and diced
    orange
1 egg, beaten
½ teaspoon grated orange
    peel
1 (2½- to 3-pound) boneless
    center cut loin pork roast
¼ cup currant jelly
1 tablespoon cranberry
    liqueur or cassis

Toss cranberries with sugar in small bowl; set aside. Melt butter in saucepan over medium heat until foamy. Add onion; cook and stir until tender. Remove from heat. Combine stuffing mix, broth, orange, egg and orange peel. Add cranberry mixture and onion; toss lightly.

Preheat oven to 325°F. To butterfly roast, cut lengthwise down roast almost to, but not through bottom. Open like a book. Cover roast with plastic wrap; pound with flat side of meat mallet. Remove plastic wrap; spread roast with part of stuffing. Close halves together and tie roast with cotton string at 2-inch intervals. Place leftover stuffing in covered casserole; bake with roast during last 45 minutes of cooking time. Place roast on meat rack in foil-lined roasting pan.

Combine jelly and liqueur. Brush half of mixture over roast after first 45 minutes in oven. Roast 30 minutes more or until internal temperature reaches 165°F when tested with meat thermometer inserted into thickest part of roast. Brush with remaining jelly mixture. Transfer roast to cutting board; cover with foil. Let stand 10 to 15 minutes before carving. Internal temperature will continue to rise 5°F to 10°F during stand time. Carve roast crosswise; serve with stuffing.

Makes 8 to 10 servings

*Glazed Roast Pork Loin
with Cranberry Stuffing*

KITCHEN TOOL TIME

ROASTING PAN

Remember the dark-blue, speckled enamel roasting pan your mom or grandma pulled out of hiding every Thanksgiving? Today that's not your only choice. Roasting pans are available in many shapes, sizes and prices. You can pay as little as $2 and as much as $300. But before you begin your quest for the perfect roasting pan, you need to determine what type of pan best suits your needs. Think about how you want to use your roasting pan and what is important to you in a pan.

Roasting pans can be great all-purpose pans ideal for much more than just roasting meat. They come in handy when roasting vegetables and potatoes, and are great when making lasagna, casseroles, crisps or cobblers for a crowd. Filled with water, they create the perfect water bath for making custards and cheesecakes.

If you plan to use your roasting pan only once a year, a disposable aluminum foil pan may be the one for you. These pans are great because they are reasonably priced and require no cleanup or storage space. Just discard them after using. When using a disposable aluminum foil pan, keep these tips in mind:

• Foil pans need extra support when cooking a heavy turkey or roast. Consider using a heavy-duty aluminum foil pan or doubling up standard aluminum foil pans. For either type, placing it on a baking sheet is a must. This will allow you to remove it from the oven without having dinner end up on the floor or all over you.

• Before making gravy from the pan drippings, pour the drippings into a saucepan as the disposable aluminum foil pans are not strong enough to be used directly over a hot burner.

If you plan to use your roasting pan for a variety of cooking needs, not just for the occasional roast, consider investing in a good quality roasting pan that will cook with you throughout the years. It may cost a little more, but it will be well worth the price. Keep the following tips in mind when choosing a roasting pan:

• The pan needs to be just large enough to hold the biggest thing you will roast without touching the sides of the pan. A larger pan will only be cumbersome and difficult to handle.

• Choose a pan that is heavy and won't buckle under the weight of a large turkey or large cut of meat. Be careful not to choose a pan that is heavier than you can lift once the food is in it.

• Strong handles are very important. Lifting a hot, heavy pan is much easier with sturdy, fixed handles.

• Consider the shape of the pan. Oval pans are perfect for cooking a single roast or turkey, but it is more difficult to use them for two smaller roasts or chickens. Rectangular pans with rounded corners, however, can accommodate a wider range of food sizes than oval pans.

• Choose a pan with sides that are about 3 inches high. If the sides are higher, the hot air may not be able to get to the bottom of the pan to cook the food evenly. If the sides are too low, the drippings can spill when pulling the pan out of the oven.

• If you make gravy with the pan drippings, be sure to get a pan that can stand up to the direct heat of a burner. Besides aluminum pans, stainless steel pans are also suitable for stove-top cooking. However, using an aluminum or stainless steel pan with a nonstick coating won't give you the crispy browned bits on the bottom of the pan that help to make a rich gravy.

Most importantly, before you purchase any roasting pan, measure the inside of your oven. Not all ovens are the same size and some will not accommodate larger roasting pans. Pans should have 2 inches of air space on all sides when in the oven to allow good air circulation.

Harvest Pot Roast with Sweet Potatoes

▌▌▌

1 envelope LIPTON® RECIPE
   SECRETS® Onion Soup
   Mix
1½ cups water
   ¼ cup soy sauce
2 tablespoons firmly packed
   dark brown sugar
1 teaspoon ground ginger
   (optional)
1 (3- to 3½-pound) boneless
   pot roast (rump, chuck or
   round)
4 large sweet potatoes,
   peeled, if desired, and
   cut into large chunks
3 tablespoons water
2 tablespoons all-purpose
   flour

1. Preheat oven to 325°F. In Dutch oven or 5-quart heavy ovenproof saucepot, combine soup mix, water, soy sauce, sugar and ginger; add roast.

2. Cover and bake 1 hour 45 minutes.

3. Add potatoes and bake covered an additional 45 minutes or until beef and potatoes are tender.

4. Remove roast and potatoes to serving platter and keep warm; reserve juices.

5. In small cup, with wire whisk, blend water and flour. In Dutch oven, add flour mixture to reserved juices. Bring to a boil over high heat. Boil, stirring occasionally, 2 minutes. Serve with roast and potatoes.
Makes 6 servings

Honey Glazed Ham

▌▌▌

2 (8-ounce) fully-cooked ham
   steaks
¼ cup honey
3 tablespoons water
1½ teaspoons dry mustard
½ teaspoon ground ginger
¼ teaspoon ground cloves

Pan-fry or broil ham steaks until lightly browned and thoroughly heated. Remove ham from skillet or broiler pan. Combine honey, water and spices; add to pan drippings and bring to a boil. Simmer 1 to 2 minutes. Brush over ham. Serve ham with remaining sauce. *Makes 4 servings*

Favorite recipe from **National Honey Board**

*Harvest Pot Roast
with Sweet Potatoes*

Family Swiss Steak and Potatoes

▮▮▮

½ cup all-purpose flour
1½ teaspoons salt
½ teaspoon pepper
2½ pounds round steak, about 1½ inches thick
2 tablespoons CRISCO® Oil
2 cups sliced onion
1 can (14½ ounces) whole tomatoes, undrained and cut up
½ cup water
½ teaspoon dried thyme leaves
1 bay leaf
8 medium potatoes, peeled and cut in half

1. Combine flour, salt and pepper in shallow dish. Add meat. Coat both sides with flour mixture. Pound flour into meat.

2. Heat oil in large skillet or Dutch oven on medium heat. Add meat. Brown both sides, adding onion during last 2 to 3 minutes.

3. Add tomatoes, water, thyme and bay leaf. Bring to a boil. Reduce heat to low. Cover. Simmer one hour 15 minutes. Turn meat over. Add potatoes. Simmer until meat and potatoes are tender.

4. Arrange meat and potatoes on platter. Remove bay leaf from sauce. Pour sauce over meat and potatoes.

Makes 8 servings

Rosemary Roasted Chicken and Potatoes

▮▮▮

1 BUTTERBALL® Fresh Young Roaster, giblets removed
3 cloves garlic, minced
Grated peel and juice of 1 lemon
2 tablespoons vegetable oil
1 tablespoon fresh rosemary leaves
1 teaspoon cracked black pepper
¼ teaspoon salt
6 medium potatoes, cut into pieces

Preheat oven to 425°F. Mix garlic, lemon peel, lemon juice, oil, rosemary, pepper and salt in medium bowl. Place chicken, breast side up, in lightly oiled large roasting pan. Place potatoes around chicken. Drizzle garlic mixture over chicken and onto potatoes. Bake 20 to 25 minutes per pound or until internal temperature reaches 180°F in thigh. Stir potatoes occasionally to brown evenly. Let chicken stand 10 minutes before carving. *Makes 8 servings*

Roast Chicken Spanish Style

▌▌▌

1 (4½- to 5-pound) whole
   roasting chicken
   Salt and freshly ground
   black pepper
1 clove garlic, cut in half
1 tablespoon FILIPPO BERIO®
   Olive Oil
½ teaspoon dried oregano
   leaves
1 medium onion, sliced
4 plum tomatoes, diced
2 medium green bell peppers,
   seeded and cut into
   chunks
1 (10-ounce) package whole
   mushrooms, cleaned and
   trimmed

Preheat oven to 450°F. Remove and discard giblets and neck from chicken. Rinse chicken under cold water; drain well and pat dry with paper towels. Sprinkle inside and outside of chicken with salt and black pepper. Rub outside of chicken with garlic. In small bowl, combine olive oil and oregano; brush over outside of chicken. Place chicken, breast side up, in shallow roasting pan. Roast 30 minutes or until skin is browned. *Reduce oven temperature to 375°F.* Add onion and tomatoes. Cover pan with foil; bake an additional 1 hour to 1 hour and 15 minutes or until legs move freely and juices run clear, adding bell peppers and mushrooms about 20 minutes before chicken is done. Let stand 10 minutes before carving.

Makes 6 servings

Seasoned Pork Roast with Potatoes

▌▌▌

2 teaspoons LAWRY'S®
   Seasoned Salt
2 teaspoons LAWRY'S®
   Seasoned Pepper
4 teaspoons LAWRY'S® Garlic
   Salt
1 (4-pound) pork loin roast
4 medium white rose
   potatoes

Rub seasonings into roast. Place in large roasting pan, fat side up. Roast, uncovered, in 325°F. oven 45 minutes per pound. Peel potatoes and cut into ½-inch lengthwise slices. Place slices in meat drippings around roast during the last 45 minutes of roasting time. Turn potatoes once during cooking.

Makes 8 servings

Serving Suggestion: Serve potatoes and roast with your favorite vegetable and hot, crusty rolls.

COOKING CLASS 🍳

Ladle enough clear syrup from cranberry mixture into glass measuring cup to equal 1 cup.

Slice away skin from ham with utility knife.

Baked Holiday Ham with Cranberry-Wine Compote

▌▌▌

2 teaspoons peanut oil
⅔ cup chopped onion
½ cup chopped celery
1 cup red wine
1 cup honey
½ cup sugar
1 package (12 ounces) fresh cranberries
1 fully-cooked smoked ham (10 pounds)
Whole cloves
Kumquats and currant leaves for garnish

1. For Cranberry-Wine Compote, heat oil in large saucepan over medium-high heat until hot; add onion and celery. Cook until tender, stirring frequently. Stir in wine, honey and sugar; bring to a boil. Add cranberries; return to a boil. Reduce heat to low; cover and simmer 10 minutes. Cool completely.

2. Carefully ladle enough clear syrup from cranberry mixture into glass measuring cup to equal 1 cup; set aside. Transfer remaining cranberry mixture to small serving bowl; cover and refrigerate.

3. Slice away skin from ham with sharp utility knife. (Omit step if meat retailer has already removed skin.)

4. Preheat oven to 325°F. Score fat on ham in diamond design with sharp utility knife; stud with whole cloves. Place ham, fat side up, on rack in shallow roasting pan.

5. Bake, uncovered, 1½ hours. Baste ham with reserved cranberry-wine syrup. Bake 1 to 2 hours more or until meat thermometer inserted into thickest part of ham, not touching bone, registers 140°F, basting with cranberry-wine syrup twice.*

Score fat on ham in diamond design.

6. Let ham stand 10 minutes before transferring to warm serving platter. Slice ham with large carving knife. Serve warm with chilled Cranberry-Wine Compote. Garnish, if desired.

Makes 16 to 20 servings

*Total cooking time for ham should be 18 to 24 minutes per pound.

Baste ham with reserved cranberry-wine syrup.

Mustard-Crusted Roast Pork

▮▮▮

3 tablespoons Dijon mustard
4 teaspoons minced garlic,
    divided
2 whole well-trimmed pork
    tenderloins, about
    1 pound each
2 tablespoons dried thyme
    leaves
1 teaspoon black pepper
½ teaspoon salt
1 pound asparagus spears,
    ends trimmed
2 red or yellow bell peppers
    (or one of each), cut
    lengthwise into ½-inch-
    wide strips
1 cup fat-free, reduced-
    sodium chicken broth,
    divided

1. Preheat oven to 375°F. Combine mustard and 3 teaspoons garlic in small bowl. Place tenderloins on waxed paper; spread mustard mixture evenly over top and sides of both tenderloins. Combine thyme, black pepper and salt in small bowl; reserve 1 teaspoon mixture. Sprinkle remaining mixture evenly over tenderloins, patting so that seasoning adheres to mustard. Place tenderloins on rack in shallow roasting pan. Roast 25 minutes.

2. Arrange asparagus and bell peppers in single layer in shallow casserole or 13×9-inch baking pan. Add ¼ cup broth, reserved thyme mixture and remaining 1 teaspoon garlic; toss to coat.

3. Roast vegetables in oven alongside pork tenderloins 15 to 20 minutes or until thermometer inserted into center of pork registers 160°F and vegetables are tender. Transfer tenderloins to carving board; tent with foil and let stand 5 minutes. Arrange vegetables on serving platter reserving juices in dish; cover and keep warm. Add remaining ¾ cup broth and juices in dish to roasting pan. Place over range top burner(s); simmer 3 to 4 minutes over medium-high heat or until juices are reduced to ¾ cup, stirring frequently. Carve tenderloin crosswise into ¼-inch slices; arrange on serving platter. Spoon juices over tenderloin and vegetables.

Makes 8 servings

Mustard-Crusted Roast Pork

Old-Fashioned

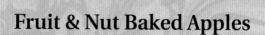

Desserts

Fruit & Nut Baked Apples

∎∎∎

- 4 large baking apples, such as Rome Beauty or Jonathan
- 1 tablespoon lemon juice
- ⅓ cup chopped dried apricots
- ⅓ cup chopped walnuts or pecans
- 3 tablespoons packed brown sugar
- ½ teaspoon ground cinnamon
- 2 tablespoons melted butter or margarine

Slow Cooker Directions

Hollow out center of each apple, leaving 1½-inch-wide cavity about ½ inch from bottom. Peel top of apple down about 1 inch. Brush peeled edges evenly with lemon juice. Mix apricots, walnuts, brown sugar and cinnamon in small bowl. Add butter; mix well. Spoon mixture evenly into apple cavities.

Pour ½ cup water in bottom of slow cooker. Place 2 apples in bottom of cooker. Arrange remaining 2 apples above but not directly on top of bottom apples. Cover and cook on LOW 3 to 4 hours or until apples are tender. Serve warm or at room temperature with caramel ice cream topping, if desired. *Makes 4 servings*

Cappuccino Cheesecake

▌▌▌

14 squares Low Fat HONEY
   MAID® Honey Grahams,
   finely crushed (about
   1 cup crumbs)
2 tablespoons margarine,
   melted
1¼ cups sugar, divided
2 (8-ounce) packages low fat
   cream cheese
1 cup egg substitute
1 tablespoon instant
   espresso powder
1 teaspoon vanilla extract

1. Mix graham crumbs, melted margarine and ¼ cup sugar in medium bowl. Press crumbs on bottom and 1-inch up side of lightly greased 9-inch springform pan.

2. Blend cream cheese and remaining 1 cup sugar in large bowl with mixer; beat in egg substitute, espresso powder and vanilla until well blended. Pour batter into prepared crust.

3. Bake in preheated 325°F oven for 55 to 60 minutes or until firm to touch. Turn oven off; cool in oven for 1 hour, leaving door ajar. Refrigerate at least 4 hours before serving.
Makes 12 servings

Strawberry Rhubarb Pie

▌▌▌

Pastry for double-crust
   9-inch pie
4 cups sliced (1-inch pieces)
   fresh rhubarb
3 cups (1 pint) fresh
   strawberries, sliced
1½ cups sugar
½ cup cornstarch
2 tablespoons quick-cooking
   tapioca
1 tablespoon grated lemon
   peel
¼ teaspoon ground allspice
1 egg, lightly beaten

Preheat oven to 425°F. Roll out half the pastry; place in 9-inch pie plate. Trim pastry; flute edges, sealing to edge of pie plate. Set aside. Place fruit in large bowl. In medium bowl, combine sugar, cornstarch, tapioca, lemon peel and allspice; mix well. Sprinkle sugar mixture over fruit; toss to coat well. Fill pie shell evenly with fruit. Roll remaining pastry to 10-inch circle. Cut into ½-inch-wide strips. Form into lattice design over fruit. Brush egg over pastry. Bake 50 minutes or until filling is bubbly and thick. Cool on wire rack. *Makes 8 servings*

Cappuccino Cheesecake

Della Robbia Cake

▐▐▐

1 package DUNCAN HINES®
    Angel Food Cake Mix
1½ teaspoons grated lemon
    peel
1 cup water
6 tablespoons granulated
    sugar
1½ tablespoons cornstarch
1 tablespoon lemon juice
½ teaspoon vanilla extract
    Few drops red food coloring
6 slices cling peaches
6 medium strawberries, sliced

Preheat oven to 375°F.

Prepare cake mix as directed on package, adding lemon peel. Bake and cool cake as directed on package.

Combine water, sugar and cornstarch in small saucepan. Cook on medium-high heat until mixture thickens and clears. Remove from heat. Stir in lemon juice, vanilla extract and food coloring.

Alternate peach slices with strawberry slices around top of cake. Pour glaze over fruit and top of cake.

Makes 12 to 16 servings

Tip: For angel food cakes, always use a totally grease-free cake pan to get the best volume.

Upside-Down German Chocolate Cake

▐▐▐

1½ cups flaked coconut
1½ cups chopped pecans
1 package DUNCAN HINES®
    Moist Deluxe German
    Chocolate or Chocolate
    Cake Mix
1 (8-ounce) package cream
    cheese, softened
½ cup butter, melted
1 pound confectioners' sugar
    (3½ to 4 cups)

Preheat oven to 350°F. Grease and flour 13×9-inch pan. Spread coconut evenly on bottom of pan. Sprinkle with pecans. Prepare cake mix as directed on package. Pour over coconut and pecans. Combine cream cheese and melted butter in medium mixing bowl. Beat at low speed with electric mixer until creamy. Add sugar; beat until blended and smooth. Drop by spoonfuls evenly over cake batter. Bake 45 to 50 minutes or until toothpick inserted halfway to bottom of cake comes out clean. Cool completely in pan. To serve, cut into individual pieces; turn upside down onto plate.

Makes 12 to 16 servings

*Upside-Down German
Chocolate Cake*

Cranberry Cobbler

▌▌▌

2 (16-ounce) cans sliced
   peaches in light syrup,
   drained
1 (16-ounce) can whole berry
   cranberry sauce
1 package DUNCAN HINES®
   Cinnamon Swirl Muffin
   Mix
½ cup chopped pecans
⅓ cup butter or margarine,
   melted
   Whipped topping or ice
   cream

Preheat oven to 350°F.

Cut peach slices in half
lengthwise. Combine peach
slices and cranberry sauce in
ungreased 9-inch square pan.
Knead swirl packet from mix for
10 seconds. Squeeze contents
evenly over fruit.

Combine muffin mix, contents
of topping packet from mix and
pecans in large bowl. Add
melted butter. Stir until
thoroughly blended (mixture
will be crumbly). Sprinkle
crumbs over fruit. Bake 40 to
45 minutes or until lightly
browned and bubbly. Serve
warm with whipped topping.
                    Makes 9 servings

Tip: Store leftovers in the
refrigerator. Reheat in
microwave oven to serve warm.

Honey Pumpkin Pie

▌▌▌

1 can (16 ounces) solid pack
   pumpkin
1 cup evaporated low-fat milk
¾ cup honey
3 eggs, slightly beaten
2 tablespoons all-purpose
   flour
1 teaspoon ground cinnamon
½ teaspoon ground ginger
½ teaspoon rum extract
   Pastry for single 9-inch pie
   crust

Combine all ingredients except
pastry in large bowl; beat until
well blended. Pour into pastry-
lined 9-inch pie plate. Bake at
400°F 45 minutes or until knife
inserted near center comes out
clean.   *Makes 8 servings*

Favorite recipe from **National
Honey Board**

Cranberry Cobbler

Bittersweet Chocolate Pound Cake

▐▐▐

CAKE

- 2 cups all-purpose flour
- 1 teaspoon baking soda
- 1 teaspoon baking powder
- 1½ cups water
- 2 tablespoons instant coffee granules
- 4 bars (2 ounces each) NESTLÉ® Unsweetened Baking Chocolate, broken up, divided
- 2 cups granulated sugar
- 1 cup (2 sticks) butter, softened
- 1 teaspoon vanilla extract
- 3 eggs

CHOCOLATE GLAZE

- 3 tablespoons butter
- 1½ cups sifted powdered sugar
- 2 to 3 tablespoons water
- 1 teaspoon vanilla extract
  Powdered sugar (optional)

Cake

COMBINE flour, baking soda and baking powder in small bowl. Bring water and coffee to a boil in small saucepan; remove from heat. *Add 3 bars (6 ounces)* baking chocolate; stir until smooth.

BEAT sugar, butter and vanilla in large mixer bowl until creamy. Add eggs; beat on high speed for 5 minutes. Beat in flour mixture alternately with chocolate mixture. Pour into well-greased 10-inch Bundt pan.

BAKE in preheated 325°F oven for 50 to 60 minutes until long wooden pick inserted into center of cake comes out clean. Cool in pan on wire rack for 30 minutes. Remove from pan; cool completely.

Chocolate Glaze

MELT *remaining* baking bar (2 ounces) and butter in small, heavy saucepan over low heat, stirring until smooth. Remove from heat. Stir in powdered sugar alternately with water until desired consistency. Stir in vanilla. Drizzle cake with Chocolate Glaze; sprinkle with powdered sugar.

Makes 12 servings

Café Mocha Shortcakes

▌▌▌

1 package (12 ounces) frozen
　pound cake, thawed, cut
　into 8 slices
3 tablespoons butter *or*
　margarine, melted
5 tablespoons freshly brewed
　coffee
1 tablespoon sugar
1¼ teaspoons ground cinnamon
1 cup KRAFT® Chocolate
　Flavored Dessert Topping
1 tub (8 ounces) COOL WHIP®
　Whipped Topping, thawed

HEAT oven to 400°F.

PLACE cake slices on baking
sheet. Stir butter, 2 tablespoons
coffee, sugar and ¼ teaspoon
cinnamon in small bowl. Brush
evenly over cake slices. Bake
8 minutes or until lightly
browned.

MIX chocolate topping,
remaining coffee and
cinnamon. Just before serving,
place one cake slice on each of
8 dessert dishes. Top evenly
with whipped topping. Drizzle
with chocolate mixture.

Makes 8 servings

Prep Time: 15 minutes

Rice Pudding Mexicana

▌▌▌

1 package instant rice
　pudding
1 tablespoon vanilla
¼ teaspoon ground cinnamon
　Dash ground cloves
¼ cup slivered almonds,
　toasted*
　Additional ground cinnamon

**To toast almonds, spread in single layer
on baking sheet. Bake in preheated
350°F oven 8 to 10 minutes or until
golden brown, stirring frequently.*

1. Prepare rice pudding
according to package directions.

2. Remove pudding from heat;
stir in vanilla, ¼ teaspoon
cinnamon and cloves. Pour
evenly into 6 individual dessert
dishes.

3. Sprinkle evenly with toasted
almonds and additional ground
cinnamon. Serve warm.

Makes 6 servings

English Bread Pudding

▐▐▐

14 slices day-old, firm-textured
    white bread (about
    12 ounces), crusts
    trimmed
1½ cups milk
  ⅓ cup butter, softened
  ⅓ cup packed light brown
    sugar
  1 teaspoon ground cinnamon
  ¼ teaspoon ground nutmeg
  ¼ teaspoon ground cloves
  1 egg
  1 package (6 ounces) mixed
    dried fruit, chopped
  1 medium apple, peeled and
    chopped
  ⅓ cup chopped nuts
    Sweetened whipped cream
    and additional ground
    nutmeg (optional)

1. Tear bread into pieces; place
in large mixing bowl. Pour milk
over bread; let soak 30 minutes.

2. Preheat oven to 350°F. Lightly
grease 9×5×3-inch loaf pan.

3. Beat butter, brown sugar,
cinnamon, nutmeg and cloves
into bread mixture with electric
mixer at low speed until
smooth, about 1 minute. Beat
in egg, dried fruit and apple.
Stir in nuts.

4. Pour mixture into prepared
pan. Bake 1 hour 15 minutes to

1 hour 30 minutes or until
toothpick inserted near center
comes out clean. Cool pudding
in pan 10 minutes. Remove
from pan; cool on wire rack
until slightly warm. Cut into
slices. Serve warm with
whipped cream and sprinkle
with nutmeg, if desired.

Makes 6 to 8 servings

Cook's Notes

If you happen to have
any of this delicious
dessert left over, store it
in the refrigerator for up
to two days. When you
are ready to indulge
again, cover and reheat
in a 350°F oven
until warm.

English Bread Pudding

Reese's® Chocolate Peanut Butter Cheesecake

▌▌▌

1¼ cups graham cracker crumbs
⅓ cup plus ¼ cup sugar
⅓ cup HERSHEY₀S Cocoa
⅓ cup butter or margarine, melted
3 packages (8 ounces each) cream cheese, softened
1 can (14 ounces) sweetened condensed milk (not evaporated milk)
1⅔ cups (10-ounce package) REESE'S® Peanut Butter Chips, melted
4 eggs
2 teaspoons vanilla extract
Chocolate Drizzle (recipe follows)
Whipped topping
HERSHEY₀S MINI KISSES™ Semi-Sweet or Milk Chocolate Baking Pieces

1. Heat oven to 300°F. Combine graham cracker crumbs, ⅓ cup sugar, cocoa and butter; press onto bottom of 9-inch springform pan.

2. Beat cream cheese and ¼ cup sugar until fluffy. Gradually beat in sweetened condensed milk, then melted chips, until smooth. Add eggs and vanilla; beat well. Pour over crust.

3. Bake 60 to 70 minutes or until center is almost set. Remove from oven. With knife, loosen cake from side of pan. Cool. Remove side of pan. Refrigerate until cold. Garnish with Chocolate Drizzle, whipped topping and Mini Kisses™. Store, covered, in refrigerator.

Makes 12 servings

Chocolate Drizzle: Melt 2 tablespoons butter in small saucepan over low heat; add 2 tablespoons HERSHEY₀S Cocoa and 2 tablespoons water. Cook and stir until slightly thickened. *Do not boil.* Cool slightly. Gradually add 1 cup powdered sugar and ½ teaspoon vanilla extract, beating with whisk until smooth. Makes about ¾ cup.

Tip: If desired, spoon drizzle into small heavy seal-top plastic bag. With scissors, make small diagonal cut in bottom corner of bag. Squeeze drizzle over top of cake.

Reese's® Chocolate Peanut Butter Cheesecake

Chocolate Toffee Crunch Fantasy

■ ■ ■

1 package DUNCAN HINES®
Moist Deluxe Devil's
Food Cake Mix
12 bars (1.4 ounces each)
chocolate covered toffee
bars, divided
3 cups whipping cream,
chilled

1. Preheat oven to 350°F. Grease and flour 10-inch tube pan.

2. Prepare, bake and cool cake following package directions. Split cake horizontally into three layers; set aside. Chop 11 candy bars into pea-size pieces (see Tip). Whip cream until stiff peaks form. Fold candy pieces into whipped cream.

3. To assemble, place one split cake layer on serving plate. Spread 1½ cups whipped cream mixture on top. Repeat with remaining layers and whipped cream mixture. Frost sides and top with remaining filling. Chop remaining candy bar coarsely. Sprinkle over top. Refrigerate until ready to serve.

Makes 12 servings

Tip: To quickly chop toffee candy bars, place a few bars in food processor fitted with steel blade. Pulse several times until pea-size pieces form. Repeat with remaining candy bars.

Serve It With Style!

This truly decadent cake is great served with a hot cup of rich coffee or tea.

Chocolate Toffee Crunch Fantasy

Strawberry Shortcake

■ ■ ■

CAKE
1 package DUNCAN HINES®
    Moist Deluxe® French
    Vanilla Cake Mix
3 eggs
1¼ cups water
½ cup butter or margarine,
    softened

FILLING AND TOPPING
2 cups whipping cream,
    chilled
⅓ cup sugar
½ teaspoon vanilla extract
1 quart fresh strawberries,
    rinsed, drained and sliced
    Mint leaves, for garnish

1. Preheat oven to 350°F. Grease two 9-inch round cake pans with butter or margarine. Sprinkle bottoms and sides with granulated sugar.

2. For cake, combine cake mix, eggs, water and butter in large bowl. Beat at low speed with electric mixer until moistened. Beat at medium speed for 2 minutes. Pour into pans. Bake at 350°F 30 to 35 minutes or until toothpick inserted in center comes out clean. Cool in pan 10 minutes. Invert onto cooling rack. Cool completely.

3. For filling and topping, place whipping cream, sugar and vanilla extract in large bowl. Beat with electric mixer on high speed until stiff peaks form. Reserve ⅓ cup for garnish. Place one cake layer on serving plate. Spread with half of whipped cream and half of sliced strawberries. Place second layer on top of strawberries. Spread with remaining whipped cream and top with remaining strawberries. Dollop with reserved ⅓ cup whipped cream and garnish with mint leaves. Refrigerate until ready to serve.

Makes 12 servings

Cook's Nook

For best results when beating whipping cream, chill the bowl and beaters along with the cream before you begin. The cold keeps the fat in the cream solid, thus increasing the volume.

Strawberry Shortcake

Weeknight Dinner Solutions

Shell Pasta with Ham and Peas

▐▐▐

- 2 cups uncooked medium shell pasta
- 6 ounces cooked 96% fat-free ham
- 2 cups frozen peas
- 1¼ cups reduced-fat (2%) milk
- 2 cloves garlic, minced
- 1½ teaspoons dried basil leaves
- ¼ teaspoon crushed red pepper *or* ⅛ teaspoon ground red pepper
- ¼ cup (1 ounce) ⅓-less-fat cream cheese
- 2 tablespoons freshly grated Parmesan cheese

1. Cook pasta according to package directions, omitting salt; drain.

2. Cut ham into ¼-inch strips. Combine peas, milk, garlic, basil and pepper in large nonstick skillet. Bring to a boil over medium heat; reduce heat to low. Simmer, uncovered, 5 minutes. Add cream cheese; gently stir until blended. Add ham and pasta. Cook over medium heat until heated through. Sprinkle with Parmesan cheese just before serving. Garnish with red bell pepper strips and fresh basil, if desired. *Makes 4 servings*

Smoked Ham Corncakes with Bean Sauce

▌▌▌

¾ **cup yellow cornmeal**
¼ **cup plus 2 tablespoons all-purpose flour**
½ **teaspoon baking soda**
½ **teaspoon salt**
1 **cup buttermilk, divided**
2 **eggs, lightly beaten**
6 **tablespoons cream cheese, softened**
2 **ears fresh corn, shucked, kernels cut from cob and divided**
⅔ **cup chopped smoked ham**
½ **cup finely chopped fresh chives**
2 **tablespoons olive oil, divided**
1 **can (15 ounces) black beans, rinsed and drained**
1 **tablespoon balsamic vinegar**
1 **clove garlic, minced**
1 **teaspoon sugar**
¼ **teaspoon black pepper**
  Sour cream (optional)
  Tomatoes (optional)

1. Combine cornmeal, flour, baking soda and salt in large bowl; set aside.

2. Combine ¾ cup buttermilk, eggs and cream cheese in blender container. Cover; blend on low speed until smooth. Add ½ cup corn; blend on low speed until coarsely chopped. Stir buttermilk mixture, remaining corn, ham and chives into cornmeal mixture.

3. Heat 1 tablespoon oil in large nonstick skillet over high heat. Drop ¼ cup batter into hot oil; spread to 4-inch circle with wooden spoon. Cook corncake 2 to 3 minutes on each side until golden brown. Remove to paper towel. Repeat with remaining batter.

4. Combine beans, remaining ¼ cup buttermilk, remaining tablespoon oil, vinegar, garlic, sugar and pepper in blender container. Cover; blend on medium speed until smooth.

5. Heat medium saucepan over low heat. Add bean mixture. Cook and stir 8 to 10 minutes until heated through. Pour into small serving bowl.

6. Serve corncakes with bean sauce, sour cream and tomatoes, if desired. Garnish as desired.   *Makes 8 servings*

Smoked Ham Corncakes with Bean Sauce

Turkey Cazuela

###

8 ounces uncooked linguini, broken in half
1⅓ cups FRENCH'S® French Fried Onions, divided
2 cups (10 ounces) cubed cooked turkey
1 can (10¾ ounces) condensed cream of chicken soup
1 jar (8 ounces) picante sauce
½ cup sour cream
1 cup (4 ounces) shredded Cheddar cheese

Preheat oven to 350°F. Grease 2-quart shallow baking dish. Cook linguini according to package directions, using shortest cooking time. Layer linguini, ⅔ *cup* French Fried Onions and turkey in prepared baking dish.

Combine soup, picante sauce and sour cream in large bowl. Pour over turkey.

Cover; bake 40 minutes or until hot and bubbling. Stir gently. Sprinkle with cheese and remaining ⅔ *cup* onions. Bake 5 minutes or until onions are golden.

Makes 4 to 6 servings

Prep Time: 20 minutes
Cook Time: 45 minutes

Navy Bean and Ham Soup

###

1 bag (16 ounces) navy beans
1 tablespoon vegetable oil
½ cup chopped onion
½ cup chopped celery
1 pound ham, diced
2 cups water
1 can (14½ ounces) chicken broth
2 bay leaves
2½ teaspoons LAWRY'S® Seasoned Salt
2 teaspoons LAWRY'S® Garlic Powder with Parsley
¾ teaspoon LAWRY'S® Seasoned Pepper

Wash beans and soak overnight, or for at least 4 hours. Pour off water from beans and rinse thoroughly. In soup pot or Dutch oven, heat oil. Sauté onion and celery until just tender. To pot, add drained beans and remaining ingredients. Bring to a boil; reduce heat, cover and simmer 1 hour.

Makes 4 to 6 servings

Hint: Ham hocks can replace diced ham for extra flavor. Cook at least 1½ hours if hocks are used.

Angel Hair Carbonara

▌▌▌

⅔ cup milk
2 tablespoons margarine or
    butter
1 package (4.8 ounces)
    PASTA RONI® Angel Hair
    Pasta with Herbs
2 cups chopped cooked pork
    or ham
1 package (10 ounces) frozen
    peas
¼ cup sliced green onions

1. In round 3-quart
microwavable glass casserole,
combine 1½ cups water, milk
and margarine. Microwave,
uncovered, on HIGH 4 to
5 minutes or until boiling.

2. Gradually add pasta while
stirring. Separate pasta with
fork, if needed.

3. Stir in Special Seasonings.

4. Microwave, uncovered, on
HIGH 4 minutes, stirring gently
after 2 minutes. Separate pasta
with fork, if needed. Stir in
pork, frozen peas and onions.
Continue to microwave 2 to
3 minutes. Sauce will be thin,
but will thicken upon standing.

5. Let stand 3 minutes or until
desired consistency. Stir before
serving.   *Makes 4 servings*

Texas-Style Pork Barbecue

▌▌▌

2 teaspoons CRISCO® Oil
¼ cup coarsely chopped onion
1 clove garlic, minced
¾ cup chili sauce
1 tablespoon firmly packed
    light brown sugar
1 tablespoon cider vinegar
1 tablespoon molasses
1 tablespoon water
1 teaspoon lemon juice
1 teaspoon prepared mustard
¼ teaspoon liquid smoke
⅛ teaspoon cayenne pepper
⅛ teaspoon salt
¾ pound boneless pork loin,
    cooked and thinly sliced
4 onion rolls, split and
    toasted

1. Heat oil in medium
saucepan on medium heat.
Add onion and garlic. Cook
and stir until tender. Stir in
remaining ingredients except
pork and rolls. Bring to a boil.
Reduce heat to low. Simmer
15 minutes, stirring occasionally.

2. Add meat slices to saucepan.
Stir gently to coat with sauce.
Simmer 5 minutes or until meat
is thoroughly heated.

3. Place meat on bottom half of
rolls. Cover with tops of rolls.
Serve with sauce on the side.
        Makes 4 servings

Fresh Fruity Chicken Salad

▌▌▌

Yogurt Dressing (recipe
  follows)
2 cups cubed cooked chicken
1 cup cantaloupe balls
1 cup honeydew melon cubes
½ cup chopped celery
⅓ cup cashews
¼ cup sliced green onions
Lettuce leaves

Prepare Yogurt Dressing; set
aside. Combine chicken,
melons, celery, cashews and
onions in large bowl. Add
dressing; mix lightly. Cover.
Refrigerate 1 hour. Serve on bed
of lettuce.   *Makes 4 servings*

YOGURT DRESSING
¼ cup plain yogurt
3 tablespoons mayonnaise
3 tablespoons fresh lime juice
¾ teaspoon ground coriander
½ teaspoon salt
Dash of pepper

Combine ingredients in small
bowl; mix well.

Campbell's® Ham & Pasta Skillet

▌▌▌

1 can (10¾ ounces)
  CAMPBELL'S® Condensed
  Broccoli Cheese Soup
1 cup milk
1 tablespoon spicy brown
  mustard
2 cups broccoli flowerets *or*
  1 package (10 ounces)
  frozen broccoli cuts
  (2 cups)
1½ cups cooked ham strips
3 cups cooked medium shell
  macaroni (about 2 cups
  uncooked)

In medium skillet mix soup,
milk, mustard and broccoli.
Over medium heat, heat to a
boil. Reduce heat to low. Cook
5 minutes or until broccoli is
tender. Add ham and macaroni
and heat through.
      Makes 4 servings

Prep Time: 10 minutes
Cook Time: 15 minutes

Fresh Fruity Chicken Salad

Potato and Pork Frittata

███

12 ounces (about 3 cups)
    frozen hash brown
    potatoes
1 teaspoon Cajun seasoning
4 egg whites
2 whole eggs
¼ cup low-fat (1%) milk
1 teaspoon dry mustard
¼ teaspoon black pepper
10 ounces (about 3 cups)
    frozen stir-fry vegetables
⅓ cup water
¾ cup chopped cooked lean
    pork
½ cup (2 ounces) shredded
    Cheddar cheese

1. Preheat oven to 400°F. Spray baking sheet with nonstick cooking spray. Spread potatoes on baking sheet; sprinkle with Cajun seasoning. Bake 15 minutes or until hot. Remove from oven. *Reduce oven temperature to 350°F.*

2. Beat egg whites, eggs, milk, mustard and pepper in small bowl. Place vegetables and water in medium ovenproof nonstick skillet. Cook over medium heat 5 minutes or until vegetables are crisp-tender; drain.

3. Add pork and potatoes to vegetables in skillet; stir lightly. Add egg mixture. Sprinkle with

cheese. Cook over medium-low heat 5 minutes. Place skillet in oven; bake 5 minutes or until egg mixture is set and cheese is melted. *Makes 4 servings*

Chow Mein Salad

███

2 cups chopped cooked pork,
    chicken or beef
1½ cups cooked white rice
2 cups fresh bean sprouts *or*
    1 can (16 ounces) bean
    sprouts, drained
1 cup sliced celery
1 cup shredded carrots
½ cup chopped green onions
¼ to ½ cup chopped green
    bell pepper
1 cup prepared HIDDEN
    VALLEY® Original Ranch®
    salad dressing
    Black pepper (optional)
    Lettuce leaves

In large bowl, combine pork, rice, bean sprouts, celery, carrots, green onions and bell pepper. Add salad dressing and toss lightly. Season with pepper, if desired. Cover and refrigerate until ready to serve. Just before serving, line salad bowl with lettuce; spoon salad on top.
       Makes 4 to 6 servings

Potato and Pork Frittata

Greek-Style Chicken Stew

3 pounds skinless chicken breasts
All-purpose flour
Nonstick cooking spray
2 cups cubed peeled eggplant
2 cups sliced mushrooms
¾ cup coarsely chopped onion (about 1 medium)
2 cloves garlic, minced
1 teaspoon dried oregano leaves
½ teaspoon dried basil leaves
½ teaspoon dried thyme leaves
2 cups defatted low-sodium chicken broth
¼ cup dry sherry or defatted low-sodium chicken broth
¼ teaspoon salt
¼ teaspoon black pepper
1 can (14 ounces) artichoke hearts, drained
3 cups hot cooked wide egg noodles

1. Coat chicken very lightly with flour. Generously spray nonstick Dutch oven or large nonstick skillet with cooking spray; heat over medium heat until hot. Cook chicken 10 to 15 minutes or until browned on all sides. Remove chicken; drain fat from Dutch oven.

2. Add eggplant, mushrooms, onion, garlic, oregano, basil and thyme to Dutch oven; cook and stir over medium heat 5 minutes.

3. Return chicken to Dutch oven. Stir in chicken broth, sherry, salt and pepper; heat to a boil. Reduce heat to low and simmer, covered, about 1 hour or until chicken is no longer pink in center and juices run clear, adding artichoke hearts during last 20 minutes of cooking. Serve over noodles. Garnish as desired.

Makes 6 entrée servings

Cook's Nook

When purchasing eggplant, look for a firm eggplant that is heavy for its size, with a tight glossy, deeply-colored skin. The stem should be bright green. Dull skin and rust-colored spots are a sign of old age. Refrigerate unwashed eggplant in a plastic bag for up to 5 days.

Greek-Style Chicken Stew

Quick Chunky Chili

1 pound lean ground beef
1 medium onion, chopped
1 tablespoon chili powder
1½ teaspoons ground cumin
2 cans (16 ounces each) diced tomatoes, undrained
1 can (15 ounces) pinto beans, drained
½ cup prepared salsa
½ cup (2 ounces) shredded Cheddar cheese
3 tablespoons sour cream
4 teaspoons sliced black olives

Combine meat and onion in 3-quart saucepan; cook over high heat until meat is no longer pink, breaking meat apart with wooden spoon. Add chili powder and cumin; stir 1 minute or until fragrant. Add tomatoes, beans and salsa. Bring to a boil; stir constantly. Reduce heat to low, simmer, covered, 10 minutes. Ladle into bowls. Top with cheese, sour cream and olives.

Makes 4 (1½-cup) servings

Serving Suggestion: Serve with tossed green salad and cornbread muffins.

Oven Chicken & Rice

1 can (10¾ ounces) condensed cream of mushroom soup
1⅓ cups water
1 cup long-grain or converted rice
1 teaspoon dried dill weed, divided
¼ teaspoon black pepper
1 chicken (3 pounds), cut up and skinned
½ cup crushed multi-grain crackers
1 teaspoon paprika
2 tablespoons butter, melted
Fresh dill sprig for garnish

1. Preheat oven to 375°F. Mix soup, water, rice, ¾ teaspoon dill weed and black pepper in 13×9-inch baking dish. Arrange chicken pieces on top of rice mixture. Cover tightly with foil. Bake 45 minutes.

2. Sprinkle chicken pieces with crackers, paprika and remaining ¼ teaspoon dill. Drizzle with butter. Bake 5 to 10 minutes or until chicken is tender. Season to taste with salt and pepper. Garnish with dill sprig, if desired.

Makes 4 to 5 servings

Quick Chunky Chili

KITCHEN SENSE

Forget Me Not!

Tailgating is a fabulous way to cheer on your favorite team, visit with good friends, eat great food and perhaps relive your favorite school memories. But, forgetting the necessities can turn anyone's party into a flop! Everyone always remembers the food and drinks, but don't forget some other key players.

- serving utensils
- silverware
- napkins
- paper plates
- plastic or paper cups
- bottle opener
- condiments
- cooler with ice
- sunscreen
- bug repellent
- tickets to the game

Java Jive

Perk up your after-dinner coffee. For a great new taste sensation, simply stir in the following, separately or in combination:

- ground cinnamon
- ground nutmeg
- whipped cream
- caramel topping
- chocolate shavings
- hot cocoa mix
- your favorite liquor

Carving it up!

Once you have taken the time to prepare a fabulous roast, you'll want to carve it like a pro. Just follow these few simple guidelines.

• Before carving turkey or chicken, let it stand about 15 minutes. Before carving beef, pork or lamb, let it stand 10 to 20 minutes. Stand time permits the meat to finish cooking and makes it easier to carve. If the meat is carved immediately out of the oven, it loses more of its flavorful juices.

• Unless you are planning to carve at the table, place the meat on a large cutting board with a well at one end to hold the juice. (Or place a cutting board inside a shallow baking pan with a rim. The juice will collect in the baking pan.) Use a long, sharp carving knife to slice the meat and a long-handled meat fork to steady the meat while carving.

• When carving beef, pork, veal or lamb, always cut across the grain. This gives you a more tender slice of meat.

Food Storage Safety

Enjoying wonderful food can be one of life's greatest and simplest pleasures. Ensure your family's safety by always handling and storing food properly.

Never buy canned foods that have dents or are sticky. Store them away from direct heat and light. Store new cans and dried foods behind old ones so you use the older ones first. To be on the safe side, try to use canned foods within a year of purchasing them.

Store perishables directly in the refrigerator or freezer as soon as you get home from the grocery store to ensure freshness and prevent any bacterial growth. Don't use any food that has been stored past the time it should be used. Refrigerator temperature should be 40°F and the freezer should be 0°F. Check the temperatures often with a thermometer. Don't overcrowd food since air circulation is necessary for even temperatures.

Tailgating fun

Bacon-Wrapped Bratwurst

■ ■ ■

8 links HILLSHIRE FARM® Bratwurst
2 tablespoons mustard
2 tablespoons chopped onion
2 slices Muenster cheese, each cut into 4 strips
8 slices HILLSHIRE FARM® Bacon, partially cooked and
   drained
   Prepared barbecue sauce
8 hot dog buns, toasted

Prepare grill for cooking. Slit Bratwurst lengthwise ¾ inch
deep. Evenly spread mustard inside each slit; evenly insert
onion and cheese strips. Wrap each bratwurst with 1 slice
Bacon; secure with toothpick. Grill 10 minutes, turning
frequently and brushing with barbecue sauce. When bacon
is crisp, remove toothpicks. Serve in buns.

Makes 4 servings

Chili Corn Soup

▮▮▮

2 tablespoons vegetable oil
2 medium potatoes, diced
1 medium onion, diced
1 tablespoon chili powder
1 (16-ounce) can red kidney
   beans, drained and rinsed
1 (15¼-ounce) can corn,
   drained
1 (13¾-ounce) can vegetable
   broth
1½ teaspoons TABASCO® brand
   Pepper Sauce
1 teaspoon salt

Heat oil in 4-quart saucepan over medium heat. Add potatoes and onion; cook about 5 minutes, stirring occasionally. Add chili powder; cook 1 minute, stirring frequently.

Stir in beans, corn, vegetable broth, TABASCO® Sauce and salt. Heat to boiling over high heat. Reduce heat to low; cover and simmer 15 to 20 minutes or until potatoes are tender, stirring occasionally.

Makes 6 servings

Downhome Cornsticks

▮▮▮

⅔ cup yellow or blue cornmeal
⅓ cup all-purpose flour
3 tablespoons sugar
1½ teaspoons baking powder
½ teaspoon LAWRY'S®
   Seasoned Salt
1 cup milk
2 tablespoons melted butter
1 egg, well beaten
2 tablespoons diced green
   chiles

In medium bowl, combine cornmeal, flour, sugar, baking powder and Seasoned Salt. Add mixture of milk, butter and egg; blend well. Add chiles. Spoon batter into lightly greased corn shaped molds. Bake in 425°F. oven on lowest rack 20 to 25 minutes.

Makes 12 cornsticks

Presentation: Serve warm with whipped honey butter.

Blue Cheese Burgers with Red Onion

▌▌▌

2 pounds ground chuck
2 cloves garlic, minced
1 teaspoon salt
½ teaspoon black pepper
4 ounces blue cheese
⅓ cup coarsely chopped walnuts, toasted
1 torpedo (long) red onion *or* 2 small red onions, sliced into ⅜-inch-thick rounds
2 baguettes (each 12 inches long)
Olive or vegetable oil

Combine beef, garlic, salt and pepper in medium bowl. Shape meat mixture into 12 oval patties. Mash cheese and blend with walnuts in small bowl. Divide cheese mixture equally; place onto center of 6 meat patties. Top with remaining meat patties; tightly pinch edges together to seal in filling.

Oil hot grid to help prevent sticking. Grill patties and onion slices, if desired, on covered grill, over medium KINGSFORD® Briquets, 7 to 12 minutes for medium doneness, turning once. Cut baguettes into 4-inch lengths; split each piece and brush cut side with olive oil. Move cooked burgers to edge of grill to keep warm. Grill bread, oil side down, until lightly toasted. Serve burgers and onion slices on toasted baguettes.

Makes 6 servings

Nutty Cheese Crock

▌▌▌

1 cup shredded Cheddar cheese (4 ounces)
¾ cup margarine or butter, softened
½ cup grated Parmesan cheese
¼ cup GREY POUPON® Dijon Mustard
¼ cup PLANTERS® Walnuts, chopped
2 cloves garlic, crushed
RITZ Crackers

1. Blend all ingredients except crackers in medium bowl with mixer. Refrigerate until serving time.

2. Let stand 10 minutes at room temperature before serving. Serve as a spread on crackers.

Makes 2¾ cups

Prep Time: 15 minutes
Total Time: 15 minutes

Blue Cheese Burger with Red Onion

The Famous Lipton® California Dip

▌▌▌

1 envelope LIPTON® RECIPE
SECRETS® Onion Soup
Mix
1 container (16 ounces)
regular or light sour
cream

1. In medium bowl, blend all ingredients; chill at least 2 hours.

2. Serve with your favorite dippers.

Makes about 2 cups dip

Tip: For a creamier dip, add more sour cream.

Sensational Spinach Dip: Add 1 package (10 ounces) frozen chopped spinach, thawed and squeezed dry.

California Seafood Dip: Add 1 cup finely chopped cooked clams, crabmeat or shrimp, ¼ cup chili sauce and 1 tablespoon horseradish.

California Bacon Dip: Add ⅓ cup crumbled cooked bacon or bacon bits.

California Blue Cheese Dip: Add ¼ pound crumbled blue cheese and ¼ cup finely chopped walnuts.

Hot Mulled Cider

▌▌▌

½ gallon apple cider
½ cup packed light brown
sugar
1½ teaspoons balsamic or cider
vinegar
1 teaspoon vanilla
1 cinnamon stick
6 whole cloves
½ cup applejack or bourbon
(optional)

Slow Cooker Directions
Combine all ingredients in slow cooker. Cover and cook on LOW 5 to 6 hours. Discard cinnamon stick and cloves. Serve in hot mugs. *Makes 16 servings*

Cook's Notes

In hot weather, food should never sit out for over 1 hour. A great way to keep a dip cold while at the big game is to set the bowl of dip in a bowl of ice.

The Famous Lipton®
California Dip

Spicy Southwest Corn Cheese Soup

▌▌▌

- 1 package (10 ounces) frozen sweet corn, thawed, drained
- 1 clove garlic, minced
- 1 tablespoon butter or margarine
- ¾ pound (12 ounces) VELVEETA® Pasteurized Prepared Cheese Product, cut up
- 1 can (4 ounces) chopped green chilies
- ¾ cup chicken broth
- ¾ cup milk
- 2 tablespoons chopped fresh cilantro

1. Cook and stir corn and garlic in butter in large saucepan on medium-high heat until tender. Reduce heat to medium.

2. Stir in remaining ingredients; cook until Velveeta is melted and soup is thoroughly heated. Top each serving with crushed tortilla chips, if desired.

Makes 4 (1-cup) servings

A Taste of Nutrition: A serving of Spicy Southwest Corn Cheese Soup is high in calcium. In addition, it is also an excellent source of vitamins A and C.

Prep Time: 15 minutes
Cook Time: 10 minutes

Southwestern Potato Salad

▌▌▌

- 5 large red or white potatoes (about 2 pounds total)
- ¼ pound bacon
- ½ cup diced green chilies, drained
- ⅓ cup chopped parsley
- ¼ cup finely chopped onion
- ⅓ cup vegetable oil
- 3 tablespoons white wine vinegar
- ½ teaspoon salt
- ¼ teaspoon black pepper
- ¼ teaspoon ground cumin
- 3 drops hot pepper sauce

Place potatoes in large saucepan with 2 inches of boiling water. Cook, covered, 20 to 25 minutes or until tender. Drain and let stand until cool. Meanwhile, place bacon in large skillet; cook over medium-high heat until crisp. Drain bacon on paper towels. Let cool slightly; crumble. Cut potatoes into cubes; place in large bowl. Add bacon, chilies, parsley and onion; mix lightly. Whisk remaining ingredients in small bowl until well blended. Pour over potato mixture; toss gently to coat potatoes evenly. Cover and refrigerate 2 hours for flavors to blend.

Makes 6 to 8 servings

Spicy Southwest Corn Cheese Soup

Cranberry Scones

▮▮▮

1½ cups all-purpose flour
½ cup oat bran
¼ cup plus 1 tablespoon sugar, divided
2 teaspoons baking powder
½ teaspoon baking soda
½ teaspoon salt
5 tablespoons cold margarine or butter
¾ cup dried cranberries
⅓ cup milk
1 egg
¼ cup sour cream
1 tablespoon uncooked old-fashioned or quick oats (optional)

Preheat oven to 425°F. Combine flour, oat bran, ¼ cup sugar, baking powder, baking soda and salt in large bowl. Cut in margarine with pastry blender or 2 knives until mixture resembles coarse crumbs. Stir in cranberries. Lightly beat milk and egg in small bowl. Reserve 2 tablespoons milk mixture; set aside. Stir sour cream into remaining milk mixture. Stir into flour mixture until soft dough forms.

Turn out dough onto well-floured surface. Gently knead 10 to 12 times. Roll out into 9×6-inch rectangle. Cut dough into 6 (3-inch) squares using floured knife; cut diagonally into halves, forming 12 triangles. Place 2 inches apart on ungreased baking sheets. Brush triangles with reserved milk mixture. Sprinkle with oats, if desired, and remaining 1 tablespoon sugar.

Bake 10 to 12 minutes or until golden brown. Remove from baking sheets and cool on wire racks 10 minutes. Serve warm.

Makes 12 scones

Cook's Nook

Scones are similar to biscuits, but the dough is richer due to the addition of cream and eggs. While the dough can be cut into any shape, scones are usually cut into wedges or triangles. They are traditionally served with butter, preserves and whipped cream.

Cranberry Scones

Rise and Shine Muffins

■ ■ ■

1 cup high fiber bran cereal, crushed
⅔ cup skim milk
1 cup coarsely grated apple
⅔ cup brown sugar
½ cup coarsely grated zucchini
½ cup coarsely grated carrots
½ cup crunchy peanut butter
1 teaspoon maple extract
1 egg
2 egg whites
1¾ cups whole wheat flour
1 tablespoon baking powder
1 tablespoon orange peel
2 teaspoons ground cinnamon
1 teaspoon lite salt
   Cooking spray

Preheat oven to 375°F. Mix bran cereal and milk in large bowl; let stand until softened. Fold in apple, brown sugar, zucchini, carrots, peanut butter and maple extract until mixed. In small bowl, beat egg and egg whites; fold into bran mixture. Combine flour, baking powder, orange peel, cinnamon and salt in medium bowl. Add dry ingredients to bran mixture, being careful not to overmix.

Spray muffin pan with nonstick cooking spray. Divide batter evenly among muffin cups. Place shallow pan of water on bottom rack of oven to prevent muffins from drying. Place muffins on middle rack and bake 20 to 25 minutes or until golden brown. Remove from muffin pan and serve.

Makes 12 muffins

Favorite recipe from **Peanut Advisory Board**

Serve It With Style!

*F*or easy travel and a great presentation, place a colorful napkin in a plastic bowl with a lid. You can even choose school colors for the napkin to really get into the spirit. Place the muffins in the bowl and keep the lid tight until ready to serve.

Touchdown Brownie Cups

Touchdown Brownie Cups

┃┃┃

- 1 cup (2 sticks) butter or margarine
- ½ cup HERSHEY'S Cocoa or HERSHEY'S Dutch Processed Cocoa
- 1 cup packed light brown sugar
- ½ cup granulated sugar
- 3 eggs
- 1 teaspoon vanilla extract
- 1 cup all-purpose flour
- 1⅓ cups chopped pecans, divided

1. Heat oven to 350°F. Line 2½-inch muffin cups with paper or foil bake cups.

2. Place butter in large microwave-safe bowl; cover. Microwave at HIGH (100%) 1½ minutes or until melted. Add cocoa; stir until smooth. Add brown sugar and granulated sugar; stir until well blended. Add eggs and vanilla; beat well. Add flour and 1 cup pecans; stir until well blended. Fill prepared muffin cups about ¾ full with batter; sprinkle about 1 teaspoon remaining pecans over top of each.

3. Bake 20 to 25 minutes or until tops begin to dry and crack on top. Cool completely in cups on wire rack.

Makes about 17 cupcakes

Magic Cookie Bars

▌▌▌

½ cup (1 stick) butter or
  margarine
1½ cups graham cracker
  crumbs
1 (14-ounce) can EAGLE®
  BRAND Sweetened
  Condensed Milk (NOT
  evaporated milk)
2 cups (12 ounces) semi-
  sweet chocolate chips
1⅓ cups flaked coconut
1 cup chopped nuts

1. Preheat oven to 350°F (325°F for glass dish). In 13×9-inch baking pan, melt butter in oven.

2. Sprinkle crumbs over butter; pour **Eagle Brand** evenly over crumbs. Layer evenly with remaining ingredients; press down firmly.

3. Bake 25 minutes or until lightly browned. Cool. Chill if desired. Cut into bars. Store loosely covered at room temperature.
Makes 24 to 36 bars

7-Layer Magic Cookie Bars:
Substitute 1 cup (6 ounces) butterscotch-flavored chips for 1 cup semi-sweet chocolate chips and proceed as directed above.

Magic Peanut Cookie Bars:
Substitute 2 cups (about ¾ pound) chocolate-covered peanuts for semi-sweet chocolate chips and chopped nuts.

Magic Rainbow Cookie Bars:
Substitute 2 cups plain candy-coated chocolate candies for semi-sweet chocolate chips.

Bake Time: 25 minutes

Cook's Notes

Try cutting bar cookies into triangles or diamonds for fun new shapes. To make serving easy, remove a corner piece first; then remove the rest.

Magic Cookie Bars and Magic Rainbow Cookie Bars

Caramel Oatmeal Chewies

▌▌▌

1¾ cups quick or old-fashioned
   oats
1¾ cups all-purpose flour,
   divided
¾ cup packed brown sugar
½ teaspoon baking soda
¼ teaspoon salt (optional)
¾ cup (1½ sticks) butter or
   margarine, melted
1 cup chopped nuts
2 cups (12-ounce package)
   NESTLÉ® TOLL HOUSE®
   Semi-Sweet Chocolate
   Morsels
1 cup caramel ice-cream
   topping

COMBINE oats, 1½ cups flour, brown sugar, baking soda and salt in large bowl; stir to break up brown sugar. Stir in butter, mixing until well blended. Reserve *1 cup* oat mixture; press remaining oat mixture onto bottom of greased 13×9-inch baking pan.

BAKE in preheated 350°F. oven for 10 to 12 minutes or until light brown; cool on wire rack for 10 minutes. Sprinkle with nuts and morsels. Mix caramel topping with remaining flour in small bowl; drizzle over morsels to within ¼ inch of pan edges. Sprinkle with reserved oat mixture.

BAKE at 350°F. for 18 to 22 minutes or until golden brown. Cool in pan on wire rack; chill until firm.

Makes about 2½ dozen bars

Cook's Nook

For easy removal of brownies and bar cookies (and no cleanup!), line the baking pan with foil and leave at least 3 inches hanging over on each end. Use the foil to lift out the brownies or bars, place on a cutting board and carefully remove the foil. Cut the treats into pieces.

ACKNOWLEDGMENTS

The publisher would like to thank the companies and organizations listed below for the use of their recipes and photographs in this publication.

Blue Diamond Growers®

Butterball® Turkey Company

Campbell Soup Company

ConAgra Grocery Products Company

Duncan Hines® and Moist Deluxe® are registered trademarks of Aurora Foods Inc.

Eagle® Brand

Filippo Berio Olive Oil

Fleischmann's® Original Spread

The Golden Grain Company®

Grey Poupon® Dijon Mustard

Hershey Foods Corporation

Hillshire Farm®

HONEY MAID® Honey Grahams

The HV Company

The Kingsford Products Company

Kraft Foods, Inc.

Lawry's® Foods, Inc.

Lipton®

McIlhenny Company (TABASCO® brand Pepper Sauce)

National Cattlemen's Beef Association

National Honey Board

Nestlé USA, Inc.

Peanut Advisory Board

The Procter & Gamble Company

Reckitt Benckiser

INDEX

Angel Hair Carbonara, 67

Bacon-Wrapped Bratwurst, 78
Baked Holiday Ham with Cranberry-Wine Compote, 40
Beef & Artichoke Casserole, 16
Bittersweet Chocolate Pound Cake, 52
Blue Cheese Burgers with Red Onion, 82
Broccoli Casserole with Crumb Topping, 2
Broccoli-Rice Casserole, 24

Café Mocha Shortcakes, 53
California Bacon Dip, 84
California Blue Cheese Dip, 84
California Seafood Dip, 84
Campbell's® Ham & Pasta Skillet, 68
Cappuccino Cheesecake, 46
Caramel Oatmeal Chewies, 94
Chicken & Biscuits, 14
Chili Corn Soup, 80
Chocolate Drizzle, 56
Chocolate Toffee Crunch Fantasy, 58
Chow Mein Salad, 70
Cranberry Cobbler, 50
Cranberry-Raisin Stuffing, 13
Cranberry Scones, 88
Creamed Spinach, 13
Creamy Chicken and Pasta with Spinach, 18

Della Robbia Cake, 48
Downhome Cornsticks, 80

English Bread Pudding, 54

Family Swiss Steak and Potatoes, 38
Fresh Fruity Chicken Salad, 68

Fruit & Nut Baked Apples, 44

Garden Vegetable Salad, 4
Georgia-Style Lemon Pilaf, 12
Glazed Roast Pork Loin with Cranberry Stuffing, 32
Greek-Style Chicken Stew, 72
Green Beans and Shiitake Mushrooms, 10

Harvest Pot Roast with Sweet Potatoes, 36
Herb Roasted Turkey, 28
Honey Glazed Ham, 36
Honey Pumpkin Pie, 50
Hot Mulled Cider, 84

Italian-Style Meat Loaf, 31

Magic Cookie Bars, 92
Magic Peanut Cookie Bars, 92
Magic Rainbow Cookie Bars, 92
Mandarin Orange and Red Onion Salad, 4
Mexican Lasagna, 24
Mustard-Crusted Roast Pork, 42

Navy Bean and Ham Soup, 66
Nutty Cheese Crock, 82

Oven Chicken & Rice, 74

Peppered Beef Tip Roast, 31
Pork Chops and Apple Stuffing Bake, 30
Potato and Pork Frittata, 70

Quick Chunky Chili, 74

Reese's® Chocolate Peanut Butter Cheesecake, 56
Reuben Noodle Bake, 20
Rice Pudding Mexicana, 53

Rise and Shine Muffins, 90
Roast Chicken Spanish Style, 39
Roasted Idaho & Sweet Potatoes, 12
Roasted Mixed Vegetables, 6
Rosemary Roasted Chicken and Potatoes, 38

Seasoned Pork Roast with Potatoes, 39
Sensational Spinach Dip, 84
7-Layer Magic Cookie Bars, 92
Shell Pasta with Ham and Peas, 62
Smoked Ham Corncakes with Bean Sauce, 64
Southwestern Potato Salad, 86
Spicy Southwest Corn Cheese Soup, 86
Spinach, Cheese & Walnut Salad, 8
Spinach-Potato Bake, 22
Strawberry Rhubarb Pie, 46
Strawberry Shortcake, 60
Swanson® Glazed Snow Peas & Carrots, 6
Sweet Potato and Apple Casserole, 26

Texas-Style Pork Barbecue, 67
The Famous Lipton® California Dip, 84
Touchdown Brownie Cups, 91
Tuna Noodle Casserole, 22
Turkey Cazuela, 66
Turnip Shepherd's Pie, 20
Tuscan Pot Pie, 16
Twice Baked Ranch Potatoes, 8

Upside-Down German Chocolate Cake, 48

Yogurt Dressing, 68